"It's real!" This is what Tina scribbled on a piece of paper when she regained consciousness to let her family know that Heaven is real!

ACKNOWLEDGEMENTS

To the God of the universe, who has revealed Himself in Jesus, as He has given me a deeper understanding of the HOPE of eternity and the HOPE of heaven... I'm so humbled and honored that HE continues to show me how "IT'S REAL"... He is real... Heaven is real...

To my husband of 34 years -
Brian, may you know and understand the depth of strength, hope and love, that I've experienced with you in over three and a half decades.Your trust in our God who has every detail lined out, has put you in the front of that line in my life, heart, and soul as my best friend and life-partner.I praise God He gave me you for this life on earth, and the timing of you being able to perform life-saving CPR for me on 2/12/2018!

To my 6 priority gifts from God,
I am beyond grateful for you kids, and the manner in which you hold my heart. You are constant resources of encouragement and have loved me graciously.

To Vickie,
You have shared your expertise and wisdom in the process of this project and truly live out the Gospel for us.

INTRODUCTION

Truly... I am changed by everything I have experienced - dying without warning, visiting Heaven, seeing Jesus, miraculously returning to my body made alive by His touch. These experiences have shaped my perspective on the impossible challenges we face in a fallen world.

Having encountered the miraculous for myself, I know that we can rest in God's goodness and kindness during the most impossible trials.

I have been a follower of Jesus for many years and always believed in the reality of Heaven. Unfortunately, I have not always thought and lived like I understood its' truth.

When my body died, I found myself standing at the gates of Heaven in front of Jesus. Nothing else mattered. The overwhelming love, the peace, and the joy that radiates from Him are truly indescribable and absolutely worth everything to gain eternal life in His Presence.

I am not perfect, but I am changed. Jesus sent me back to witness to the indisputable reality of eternal life. This gift from Jesus is intended to encourage, comfort, and strengthen believers as we walk in this fallen world towards a perfect one. Heaven... It's real!

Proverbs 2: 1-8 ESV

My son, if you receive my words and treasure up my commandments with you, making your ear attentive to wisdom and inclining your heart to understanding; yes, if you call out for insight and raise your voice for understanding, if you seek it like silver and search for it as for hidden treasures, then you will understand the fear of the Lord and find the knowledge of God. For the Lord gives wisdom; from his mouth come knowledge and understanding; he stores up sound wisdom for the upright; he is a shield to those who walk in integrity, guarding the paths of justice and watching over the way of his saints.

Today I choose to change my perspective to a heavenly one regarding:

_____

_____

_____

_____

_____

_____

_____

_____

_____

_____

_____

_____

_____

_____

My thoughts…

God…..

      I will always choose the truth of Your Word and trust that You are at work in my life. In prayer, Jesus spoke to me, "How could you not, Tina? When I touched your heart after it had stopped beating for 27 minutes, it immediately was restored. I can do all things if they are according to My plans."

    I was without sign of life - no heartbeat, no breath. No reason for my family to believe for a miracle after twenty-seven minutes.   Despairing, without hope, overcome by grief. And in an instant, it all changed with one touch from the Savior.

    I pray I will be faithful in choosing to look through His eyes at life rather than through my own eyes. After dying and returning to life, I know it doesn't matter how impossible the situation seems to be. God is much more real, all-powerful, and truly sovereign than earthly eyes can comprehend. He WILL accomplish His plans and purposes.

Philippians 4:4-7 ESV

Rejoice in the Lord always; again I will say, rejoice. Let your reasonableness be known to everyone. The Lord is at hand; do not be anxious about anything, but in everything by prayer and supplication with thanksgiving let your requests be made known to God. And the peace of God, which surpasses all understanding, will guard your hearts and your minds in Christ Jesus.

Are there circumstances that you don't understand? Or don't know how to navigate through? What do you need to surrender to God's sovereignty in order to experience His peace that passes understanding?

_____

_____

_____

_____

_____

_____

_____

_____

_____

_____

_____

_____

_____

_____

_____

_____

My thoughts…

God, my strength comes from Your Sovereignty. I know it is only through You. I don't understand how I could be in great shape, working out all the time, yet have something wrong with my heart.   I don't know why it is the way it is and still has an irregular beat. But I know that You know. And You allowed this for Your purposes so that I could be a witness of You, Heaven, and eternal life. Is this flawed heart on purpose? Are You are turning something the enemy intended for evil into something wondrous?

The answer probably doesn't matter as much as the fact that I died at fifty-one years of age, and You resurrected me.   And the time spent with You in Heaven, seeing You face to face, seeing how full of beauty You are, Lord… What an immeasurable gift you have filled my flawed heart and spirit with.

I will rest in Your plans and purposes. I don't have to understand everything to delight in Your will and walk in Your ways. I choose to rest in Your peace that passes all understanding because I know WHO You are and that Your goodness and kindness never fail.

Ps. 27:13-14 ESV

I believe that I shall look upon the goodness of the Lord in the land of the living! Wait for the Lord; be strong, and let your heart take courage; wait for the Lord!

Is waiting hard for you? Do you have a tendency to try to figure it all out on your own? Knowing WHO God is - His great love towards you as your Heavenly Father - is key to waiting. God promises that all things work together for good for those who love Him and are called to His purposes (Rom. 8:28). He has your best interests at heart. You don't have to hold on so tight or have all of the answers. Intentionally get into His presence and stay there in worship. Seek Truth through His Word, listen to His voice, and rest in His promises to you - they are life to the soul! What do you need to let go of figuring out? How can you be intentional about waiting, resting, and trusting?

_____
_____
_____
_____
_____
_____
_____
_____
_____
_____
_____
_____
_____
_____

My thoughts…

WAIT on Him… REST with Him… TRUST in Him …. If I wait, I WILL get rest IN HIM. If I wait, a calmness sets in, and I can more fully trust in Him. If I wait, the lens of my spirit will bring in to focus all the good that unfolds every day through everything that God is doing all the time. He continues to reset the compass of my heart through waiting, resting, and trusting.

As I seek His Truth through Scripture, it quiets my mind and heart by the power of the Holy Spirit. I don't have to figure everything out right now. I can wait for God to reveal His plans and purposes.

Truly, through my death, return to life, and the lessons I continue to learn, I am absolutely confident that God is always good! I commit to actively and prayerfully waiting on the Lord, resting with Him, in His beautiful Presence… with my heart and mind bowed before Him. No need for a restless heart or mind. I can wait because I know WHO He is.

Ps. 100:3-5 ESV

Know that the Lord, he is God! It is he who made us, and we are his; we are his people, and the sheep of his pasture.   Enter his gates with thanksgiving, and his courts with praise! Give thanks to him; bless his name. For the Lord is good; his steadfast love endures forever, and his faithfulness to all generations.

Did you know that act of giving thanks is an invitation to enter through the gates of Heaven into God's Presence? Start each day's devotions with giving thanks. There is so much to be thankful for - not just circumstances, although they are important. Think deeply on WHO God is, HOW much He loves you, and WHAT He has done on your behalf. Journal the eternal truths you are thankful for that don't change despite circumstances. We praise Him in life's storms by knowing the WHO, HOW, and WHAT of God that is embedded in our hearts.

_____

_____

_____

_____

_____

_____

_____

_____

_____

_____

_____

_____

Day 4 - Giving Thanks

My thoughts…

How can I thank you, God? Again, I say - by living for You, through and in You, for the rest of my days on this earth.

Your miraculous goodness and kindness towards me remind me of what matters most… eternal life in Your Presence! After the indescribable joy, love, and beauty I have experienced with You in Heaven, my soul longs for a deeper relationship with You.

I've stood at Your gates in Heaven, and someday I know I will be ushered through them for eternity. For now, You promise to be with me through the gift of thanksgiving and praise. And truly, when I praise You for Your loving kindness, tender mercy, and overwhelming love, I am ushered back into Your Presence while still in this earthly vessel.

Please help me to press on towards the high calling of Heaven. I thank You for a deeper understanding of its' reality. I pray for courage and the opportunity to share the miracle You gave me so that others might find hope and faith.

2 Corinthians 5:6-9 ESV

So we are always of good courage. We know that while we are at home in the body we are away from the Lord, for we walk by faith, not by sight. Yes, we are of good courage, and we would rather be away from the body and at home with the Lord. So whether we are at home or away, we make it our aim to please him.

Are you afraid of sickness? Death? Or have you lost a loved one and the grief feels overwhelming? Do you know how to share from a biblical perspective what death truly is for the believer in Christ? Journal a biblical statement of death for Christians. Refer to this truth when fear of death or loss of loved ones impacts you or those around you. It is such a comfort to know how temporary our earthly journey is, and how wonderful eternity in Heaven will be!

_____

_____

_____

_____

_____

_____

_____

_____

_____

_____

_____

_____

_____

_____

_____

_____

My thoughts…

God… Since the day I died and met You face to face, I know without a shadow of a doubt that You are who You say You are - the Way, the Truth, and the Life. I know what death is, and I am no longer afraid. Because You conquered death, I know it is absolutely true what the Apostle Paul said that while we are at home in the body, we are away from You.

It's still hard to describe the colors of Heaven - like sunflowers and sunsets - light radiating everywhere but no sun because You are the source of light and life. When I saw You, I knew I was in Heaven with You. There was no sadness or grieving for my body that had died. Only joy - so intense - and love so overwhelming… I long to be in your Presence fully and completely.

I know You touched my dead body and my heart started beating again. I know You returned me with Your purposes to fulfill. I will share with all who will listen that death is nothing to fear for those who love You. It truly is a victory!

Matthew 13: 44-46 ESV

"The kingdom of heaven is like treasure hidden in a field, which a man found and covered up. Then in his joy he goes and sells all that he has and buys that field. "Again, the kingdom of heaven is like a merchant in search of fine pearls, who, on finding one pearl of great value, went and sold all that he had and bought it."

Do you wrestle with distraction? It's easy to get off course, focusing on the wrong priorities instead of God's priorities for us. The cares of this world rob us of a heavenly perspective, getting our attention and energies focused elsewhere instead of what is most important. Identify distractions in your life that can take you away from God's priorities. Identify tangible ways you will intentionally focus on seeking the Kingdom of God first, trusting that He will take care of the rest.

_____
_____
_____
_____
_____
_____
_____
_____
_____
_____
_____
_____
_____
_____
_____
_____
_____
_____

My thoughts…

God…You are worth everything. You know everything in my heart, mind, and soul….even the struggles that I face each and every day. You know that sometimes having a defibrillator bothers me. That sometimes, I am still afraid of my heart stopping again. You even know that sometimes I still stay hunched over from the trauma my body experienced as the paramedics and doctors were trying to revive me.

But You also know that no matter what the day-to-day emotions are, the Truth of You is steady and deep. It runs through me like a deep river as the source of strength and hope in my life. There may be storms on the surface, but there is peace in the very core of my being. I know WHO You are, that You are REAL, and that You are worth EVERYTHING!

After what I have seen and experienced, I would not trade anything this world has to offer for a moment in Your Presence, infused with Your love, peace, and joy. Worldly riches, success, a future filled with the most wonderful experiences this world has to offer. None of it compares to You. I have seen You. I have seen Heaven. You are what my heart longs for. You are worth everything. I will live for You.

Exodus 4:10-13 ESV

But Moses said to the Lord, "Oh, my Lord, I am not eloquent, either in the past or since you have spoken to your servant, but I am slow of speech and of tongue." Then the Lord said to him, "Who has made man's mouth? Who makes him mute, or deaf, or seeing, or blind? Is it not I, the Lord? Now therefore go, and I will be with your mouth and teach you what you shall speak." But he said, "Oh, my Lord, please send someone else."

Moses had already seen a bush burning but not burning up. He heard the voice of God speaking to him directly, with very specific instructions for the call God placed on Moses' life. How many of us long for such clear instructions from God! And yet, after seeing and hearing the miraculous, Moses still doubted his ability to do what God wanted him to do. What Moses did not understand at the time is that it was not his capabilities but about God equipping him to fulfill his calling. Has God called you to something, and you have hesitated, doubting your own abilities? Identify ways you may be shrinking back from God's purposes to use you. State the truths of God's provision when we step out in obedience to His plans.

_____

_____

_____

_____

_____

_____

_____

_____

_____

My thoughts…

Why me, God? I have lost loved ones, friends, and family that I prayed over for miraculous healing. They are with You now. I know they are healed in Your presence. But why me? People I love have died. I died too. Yet here I am, back in this earthly body after being in Your Presence in Heaven. Sometimes it is just too big for me to put my head around. I'm a wife. A mom. A follower of You, but I am not anyone exceptional. I have strengths and weaknesses like everyone else.

I know You started my heart beating again after twenty-seven minutes. No one could explain how I came back to life, except those who believe in miracles, who believe in You. I knew that while You didn't say anything audible when we met in Heaven, that You were sending me back to witness to the Truth of You and the beauty of Heaven. I feel a little bit like Moses…. wondering if You should have chosen someone more talented. All I can think is that You chose me because You know I would never shut up about You. You knew that I would tell anyone and everyone I see that You are absolutely WHO You say You are and that Heaven is more than we can hope for or imagine. You have given it to us as a gift from our loving Heavenly Father.

So… I trust You that You chose me. I trust You that You will teach me, equip me, and strengthen me to do what You have asked me to do until we are reunited again in Heaven. May Your Kingdom come, and Your will be done!

Matthew 6:31-33 ESV
Therefore do not be anxious, saying, 'What shall we eat?' or 'What shall we drink?' or 'What shall we wear?' For the Gentiles seek after all these things, and your heavenly Father knows that you need them all. But seek first the kingdom of God and his righteousness, and all these things will be added to you.

Nothing surprises God - He already knows what we need and promises to provide if we put His priorities first. Seeking the Kingdom of God means seeking heavenly instead of earthly priorities. God's priorities start with loving Him with our entire being, then loving others. We illustrate our love for God through obedience to Him and His Word. As we seek and obey Him, we become more like Him, living in the righteousness He graciously gives us. Keeping our thoughts eternally focused causes everything else to fall into perspective. Peace replaces worry as we learn to trust His plans and provision for our lives. What do you worry about? When framed through an eternal, biblical perspective, what do your worries look like?

_____

_____

_____

_____

_____

_____

_____

_____

_____

_____

_____

_____

My thoughts…

Jesus… how can it be that I've actually really seen You? Your face is so radiantly beautiful! And Heaven is so indescribably wondrous! How is it that You brought my dead body back to life and yet I still catch myself worrying? Worrying about the health of family and friends, about meeting financial obligations, even fearful at times of dying again.

How could I worry after all You have done? Why do I find myself running in circles in my mind trying to solve problems to calm my fears? I am sorry, Lord, and thank you for reminding me when I worry about the Truth of WHO You are and WHAT You have done for me.

I am grateful that You do not condemn me for worrying but instead gently lead me back to an eternal perspective. I don't want to stay trapped in only what I can see and understand because I know that You are not trapped in time as I am. I do not see or understand as You do but I am so grateful that You train my mind and heart to think more biblically and eternally. It is freeing me from useless worrying. Thank you for the Truth of Your provision. I can set my mind on the truth of Heaven, and the cares of this world fade back into proper perspective. Nothing is more important than spending eternity in Heaven with You!

Ephesians 4:31-32 ESV
Let all bitterness and wrath and anger and clamor and slander be put away from you, along with all malice. Be kind to one another, tenderhearted, forgiving one another, as God in Christ forgave you.

No one is perfect. We've all sinned and fallen short. Aren't we blessed that God does not view us through the lens of our sin and shortcomings? Because of the undeserved sacrifice by our perfect Savior, our sins are washed away. He sees us as spotless, without blemish, and loves us unconditionally. We didn't earn it and didn't deserve it.

Jesus endured so much and still loved. And forgave... even Judas. How can we love more like He loves? How can we learn to view other people the way God views them? Write down your relationship challenges and practical, biblical steps needed to put away wrong thoughts/attitudes about others and replace them with God's view of people.

_____

_____

_____

_____

_____

_____

_____

_____

_____

_____

_____

_____

My thoughts…

The day I died was an ordinary day. I was just standing in the driveway, waiting to go on a hike. And then I just dropped dead. When I came to in the hospital room with my family surrounding me, all I wanted was to tell them that I had seen Jesus face to face and how wondrous Heaven is. I remember how beautiful each of their faces were to me - my husband, my children…. Absolutely nothing else mattered. ALL of the cares of this world were gone entirely… I knew how deeply I loved each of them and that the day-to-day rubbing each other the wrong way, irritations, disagreements - none of it meant anything. None of it was worth it.

My perspective continues to change. I'm becoming more forgiving of hurts from friends and family. I'm letting more of the little things go, becoming more patient. I want to continue to grow in my perspective of what matters most with people and relationships.

I want to stay focused on what is good and right, and I don't want to be sidetracked into negative attitudes or judgments of others, assuming the worst or holding a grudge. Please, Lord, let me stay tenderhearted towards those I love. Help me to be quick to forgive just as You forgive me. I want to learn to love as You do…

Hebrews 4:12-13 ESV

For the word of God is living and active, sharper than any two-edged sword, piercing to the division of soul and of spirit, of joints and of marrow, and discerning the thoughts and intentions of the heart. And no creature is hidden from his sight, but all are naked and exposed to the eyes of him to whom we must give account.

Jesus didn't tackle temptation on His own. When Satan tempted Him, Jesus responded with "It is written…" quoting Old Testament Scripture. Fully man, tempted in every way and yet without sin. How did He do that? He constantly sought direction from His Heavenly Father. He had God's Word written in His heart so that He would not sin. If the Son of God used the Word of God to do the will of God, how much more do we need it?

We often lament that we do not know what God wants us to do, yet His Word is the roadmap to how we should live our lives. It is truly miraculous - indeed quickened by the Holy Spirit to leap off of the pages of our Bibles and plant its Truth into our hearts and minds. It is a lamp for our feet and a light for our paths. Do you value God's Word as His instruction to you? Do you prioritize prayerfully spending time in your Bible so you can learn to delight in His will and walk in His ways? Write down a commitment to prioritize learning daily from His Word.

_____

_____

_____

_____

_____

_____

_____

_____

My thoughts…

God…

I am so grateful for Your Word! It is just amazing how the Truth just jumps off of the pages to me! I have always believed that the Bible is Your Word and the roadmap for how to live my life. Before I died, I studied Your Word and planted it in my heart, but it was NEVER like this!!

I feel like I am DRINKING Your Word in! And when I drink it, I feel so cleansed! So renewed! My mind feels more alert, clearer. It's like taking off a set of glasses that aren't the correct prescription and putting on a pair that helps me see clearly!

Perhaps because I have no doubts about You, or the reality of Heaven, I am paying more attention to every word on every page of my Bible. I don't know. Maybe it is because I am more attuned to the work of Your Holy Spirit inside of me. I know I can't go a single day anymore without spending time in Your Word.

My time with You is so precious, and I need it so much! Thank you! Thank you for changing my mind and my heart to become more like Yours through the power of Your Word!

1 Samuel 3:8-11 ESV

And the Lord called Samuel again the third time. And he arose and went to Eli and said, "Here I am, for you called me." Then Eli perceived that the Lord was calling the boy. Therefore Eli said to Samuel, "Go, lie down, and if he calls you, you shall say, 'Speak, Lord, for your servant hears.' " So Samuel went and lay down in his place. And the Lord came and stood, calling as at other times, "Samuel! Samuel!" And Samuel said, "Speak, for your servant hears." 1Then the Lord said to Samuel, "Behold, I am about to do a thing in Israel at which the two ears of everyone who hears it will tingle.

God speaks in various ways but never contradicts His written Word. One way God speaks is to our spirits directly as we commune with Him in prayer (Acts 13:1-3). If you are hungry to hear God's voice, train your ear to listen. Quiet your mind and heart by moving to an undistracted setting. God can speak however He chooses, but He looks for listening hearts, people that want to hear His voice and follow through with what He calls them to do. Begin listening with prayerful time in God's Word. Move from there to prayer. We view prayer as a TRIP - Thanksgiving, Repentance, Intercession, and Praise. Thanksgiving and praise open the gates so we can enter His Presence, and repentance cleanses our minds and hearts. After praise - worshipping God for WHO He is - sit in silence, asking the Lord to speak His Truth into your heart and mind. Write down a plan to become an active listener to God:

_____

_____

_____

_____

_____

_____

_____

_____

My thoughts…

Lord! My time with You today was so very sweet. Thank you!! Your Presence in my quiet time was strong, and my heart and mind recognized Your voice directing me.

You are training me in Truth. Thank you! I know it is You speaking because You give me Your thoughts, not my own. They are always so much wiser than my own thoughts. I sense when You speak because You drop Your thoughts into my mind differently from how I process or think. Your thoughts are always so full, so complete, and bring such clarity and peace!

You know I don't want to strive. I don't want to share what You have done in my life to be about me at all. I just want to point to You. When I analyze decisions I need to make, I know that I need Your direction. I sense when You are nudging me too. It feels like a light bulb comes on or a door is opening. It's so hard to explain, but it is clearly from You.

Just as You spoke no audible words when we met face to face in Heaven, but I still had a clear understanding of what You were saying, I know that I don't need an audible voice to hear You speak. I am so grateful, and I need to listen to You so desperately. Thank you that You guide and direct me through Your Word, Your voice, wise counsel, divine appointments with others, and divinely orchestrated circumstances. Thank you, thank you, THANK YOU!

John 14:23-24 ESV

Jesus answered him, "Those who love me will do what I say. My Father will love them, and we will go to them and make our home with them. A person who doesn't love me doesn't do what I say. I don't make up what you hear me say. What I say comes from the Father who sent me.

Many people today say they believe in God. However, they do not view the Bible as holding moral authority over their lives. We believe that a person's commitment to God's Word indicates the condition of one's heart towards Him. Believers that love God wholeheartedly want to understand and obey His Word. They are eager to become more like Him, conforming their lives to His Word and ways.

Obeying God shows Him how very much we love Him. It illustrates how overwhelmingly grateful we are that Jesus paid the highest price for our salvation and eternity in Heaven with Him. Are there areas in your life where you are not fully loving and obeying God? Identify behaviors and write down action steps to obey God more fully.

_____
_____
_____
_____
_____
_____
_____
_____
_____
_____
_____
_____

. . . .

My thoughts…

Jesus, I love You. You know I want to obey You. I want to follow and serve You the rest of the days You give me. I owe You EVERYTHING… truly every beat of my heart and breath in my lungs are only because of Your miraculous touch. I am Your grateful daughter and will go where You lead.

I know that You breathed life back into my dead body so that I can share with anyone who will listen about how very real YOU are and Heaven is!   I understand the big picture, but some days I need help with the specifics. How do I balance family needs and ministry? Do we step out in faith without funding and trust You to provide? Is it like Peter when he stepped out of the boat onto the water, trusting that You would keep him from sinking below the waves?

I have witnessed the miraculous - the reality of coming back to life after death. WOW! Sometimes it is weird even saying it aloud or writing it down. Lazarus raised from the dead. Tina Hines… raised from the dead!!!! I know You can do anything You want to, and that nothing is too hard for You. Please direct me in the little steps as well as the big ones. I will seek You, listen, and trust You for the courage to obey because I love You with my whole heart - the one You brought back to life with just one touch!

Isaiah 55:8-9 ESV

For my thoughts are not your thoughts, neither are your ways my ways, declares the Lord. For as the heavens are higher than the earth, so are my ways higher than your ways and my thoughts than your thoughts.

There is much noise and scurrying in our world. This fast-paced life seems to be the norm, yet it is not God's plan. He ordered our days, our nights, even a day of rest. When we feel compelled to scurry, without waiting on God to give direction, we will get our best results instead of His.

God is not bound by time as we are. He is in the present and the future. He is all-knowing, and He is everywhere. Wouldn't you rather have His perspective, wisdom, provision, and blessing on your plans?

Waiting for God to answer, questioning whether we are hearing His voice, or even believing He is not speaking or answering your prayers is very hard. God allows these times of waiting to grow our faith. He always hears you, but He is not always bound to do what you want Him to do. What do you need to surrender to the Lord, knowing that He loves you and works for your good if you trust in Him?

_____
_____
_____
_____
_____
_____
_____
_____

. . . .

My thoughts…

God…

You made me, and You know exactly how I am wired! I am a DOER, and sometimes I have trouble waiting for direction or open doors. I surrender my impatience to You and ask for Your help in learning to wait and trust.

There is so much inside my heart that some days it feels like I want to burst! I want to be RUNNING forward, SHOUTING about all You have done! And yet, for two years, You have had me wait. Yes, I have shared my story and have not been silent. But the doors did not fling open wide in the way I hoped they would. Over and over, I have had to surrender my plans to Your purposes.

And now, I SEE WHY! These last two years of COVID-19, people have been afraid, sick, and have lost loved ones. They are grieving, depressed, anxious, restless…. So much struggle. I believe the message of hope and the reality of Heaven is exactly what needs to be heard. You gave me this message for SUCH A TIME AS THIS!

THANK YOU! And please help me to embrace this lesson of patiently waiting because Your plans are always SO MUCH BETTER THAN MINE!

Ephesians 4:21-24 ESV

...You have heard about him and were taught in him, as the truth is in Jesus, to put off your old self, which belongs to your former manner of life and is corrupt through deceitful desires, and to be renewed in the spirit of your minds, and to put on the new self, created after the likeness of God in true righteousness and holiness.

"That's just the way I am". How many times have you heard that tired excuse? Paul's letter to the Ephesians explains the need to put off old ways of thinking and living and put on new, godly ways to think and act.

Right thinking produces right behavior. Memorize Scripture that tells you why you do not need to fear if you are fearful. If you are quick to get angry, memorize Scripture that tells you to be quick to listen, slow to speak, and slow to become angry (James 1:19). Identify old habit patterns in your thinking that influence your behavior. Write them down, and attach a Scripture to each one. In this way, you are putting off the old and putting on the new. As the old thought pattern starts to run in your mind, speak the Scripture to the lie. Commit the Scripture to memory, and combat the lie with Truth every time it arises.

_____
_____
_____
_____
_____
_____
_____
_____
_____

My thoughts…

I was following you before I died. I didn't think I had many bad habits. Maybe overeating ice cream or Mexican food occasionally, but I was working out twice a day!

It's crazy how perspectives change after you die and come back to life!! What a wake-up call! Oh my, Lord, how your Holy Spirit is revealing old habits in me that You want me to let go of…

Yikes! I didn't realize that worry and fear are habits! Or self-doubt. But You show me that I habitually have these thought patterns running in my head. I guess that makes them habits! Thank you for showing me this truth about habits. It's not about ice cream - it is about how my habitual thinking processes lead to behaviors not based on faith. And thank you for showing me the Truth of Your Word regarding how to break old habits that do not please You.

I commit to You to put off the old habits and conform my mind and heart to the Truth of Your Word. I know that as I think truthfully, my habits will change. Thank you for renewing not just my dead body but for renewing my mind in You!

James 1:2-4 ESV

Count it all joy, my brothers, when you meet trials of various kinds, for you kow that the testing of yor faith produces steadfastness. And let steadfastness have its full effect, that you may be perfect and complete, lacking in nothing.

The Apostle James was writing to Jewish believers scattered across the Roman Empire. At the time of the writing, persecution was commonplace - both from Jews who did not believe in Jesus and governments that saw Christianity as a threat to their authority.

The persecution many believers face today is difficult for believers in first-world countries to imagine. Risking life to follow Jesus puts a different perspective on self-pity. What we learn from James' admonition is that trials are growth opportunities. A biblical view of the trials we face can change us from complaining to embracing the peace and joy that only comes from becoming more like Jesus. Do you struggle with self-pity? Write down the circumstances. Then, articulate a biblical response to them so that your heart and mind can be transformed when you face trials.

_____
_____
_____
_____
_____
_____
_____
_____
_____
_____

My thoughts…

Jesus, how can I, for ONE SECOND, even think, "Poor me?" And yet, I catch myself doing that sometimes still! After all You have done for me, I just don't get how those thoughts still pop up in my head.

Some days I wish my life was not so hectic, that I didn't have to have a job while raising our children. I wish I could be home, unhurried, doing what I believe You have called me to do. Sometimes I wish my grown-up children lived closer. I envy families who have their adult children and grandchildren all around them.

I find myself wanting what I do not have, and I am so sorry, God. I know the Apostle Paul made tents during his missionary journeys to support his ministry and that his life was very hectic. I only want to serve You. My personal sacrifices are so small compared to so many believers in the Early Church and today in countries where they are persecuted.

I know my circumstances are all filtered through Your loving hands. The difficult ones are intended as growth opportunities to become more like You! Forgive me when I get a case of the "poor me's". Thank you for always returning me back to the most important priorities of being faithful to Your calling to proclaim that Heaven is REAL so I can hear You say, "Well done, good and faithful servant!"

1 Thessalonians 5:16-18 ESV
Rejoice always, pray without ceasing, give thanks in all circumstances; for this is the will of God in Christ Jesus for you.

The Greek word translated "without ceasing" means constantly or without intermission. The NIV translates the word as "continually". In his letter to the Thessalonians, the Apostle Paul exhorts the believers to learn to pray continually. This was different than Jewish tradition with its' set times for prayer. The Christian is to remain in a constant state of prayer.

To pray continually, we must train ourselves to give every circumstance to Him as we go through the day. A homeless person on a street corner, a friend in need, our brothers and sisters in persecuted countries, wisdom as we interact under challenging circumstances, and with our spouses, children, friends, neighbors... The list goes on and on - there is no end to the need around us.

Describe a tangible plan to train yourself to pray without ceasing. For example, sticky notes on your desk, your dashboard, your refrigerator... reminders set in your calendar that train you to return to the Lord's Presence. Your method doesn't matter. Your faithfulness does.

_____
_____
_____
_____
_____
_____
_____

My thoughts…

When I was in Heaven, I knew that past the gates, wonderful worship was taking place and that every prayer of every saint around the world was being heard! And, Jesus was standing right there before me, yet at the same time listening and answering millions of prayers as our Mediator.

Scripture tells us to pray without ceasing. How can I do that and be present in my everyday responsibilities? Clearly, I cannot do what Jesus does, but I do believe God would not ask us to do something He did not equip us for.

I think the answer is in how God made our brains! He wired us with the capability to think conscious and subconscious thoughts at the same time! I am training myself to be praying at all times, habitually, so that it happens even when I don't think about it. It feels like driving home from work sometimes when I am on "auto-pilot". I am continuously returning to the Lord throughout the day to say thank you, seek direction, and intercede for someone as they come to my mind. My spirit can pray, and my mind can still drive a car, work on the computer, etc.

Training myself to respond with prayer to each situation means keeping my thoughts centered on God at work all around me. By training my mind to continuous prayer, I can recognize His voice better and respond to His nudge when He wants me to step forward to minister to someone.

John 8:12 ESV
Again Jesus spoke to them, saying, "I am the light of the world. Whoever follows me will not walk in darkness, but will have the light of life."

Jesus was speaking to the Pharisees. The majority of them would reject Him, but Jesus still boldly proclaimed the truth and the offer of eternal life.

The Greek word for light in this passage is "phos", and its use here denotes the source of light, truth, knowledge, and spiritual purity. In contrast, darkness here is "skotia", referring to a brand of moral darkness and its' associated wickedness.

We are called to be a light and source of Truth, shining the way out of moral darkness. It is God's heart that none would perish. Are you faithful to be a source of light in a morally dark world, sharing with all despite their possible responses? Does fear of rejection hinder your boldness? Or potential backlash? Identify barriers to faithfully witnessing to others. Biblically refute the barriers (ex: I am afraid of backlash. Biblical response: "Do not fear those who kill the body but cannot kill the soul. Rather fear him who can destroy both soul and body in hell" (Matt. 10:28).

_____
_____
_____
_____
_____
_____
_____
_____

My thoughts…

One of the things most vividly etched in my mind about Heaven is the color. Heaven was the color of sunlight - beautiful like sunflowers, soft like butter. Everything radiated this beautiful, delicate color! And then I realized - I was looking at the actual source of the light - Jesus! His face shone like the sun, and the love radiating from His Presence was so tangible.

The Creator is the Source of true Light, and He is the real Light of the World! I can't believe I was standing before Him. It is still so wondrous to me. There was no need for a sun, moon, or stars to dispel darkness. There is ABSOLUTELY NO DARKNESS in Heaven!! Such pure, clear, radiant light - indescribably beautiful!

In my devotional time, God reminded me that while He is the true Light, I am called to be a reflection of His Light to a dark world that seems to be getting darker by the day.

What does that mean for me to be a light? His light dispels darkness and gives life. As I share the truth about Jesus and the reality of Heaven, I pray people would be drawn to the Light of the World so that they, too, no longer have to walk in darkness. As I walk in purity according to Your Word, Your light can shine more brightly through me. Lord, please help me be the witness to Your Light, sharing the Way with others so they can move from darkness to Light by Your saving grace..

Colossians 1:9-11 ESV
And so, from the day we heard, we have not ceased to pray for you, asking that you may be filled with the knowledge of his will in all spiritual wisdom and understanding, so as to walk in a manner worthy of the Lord, fully pleasing to him: bearing fruit in every good work and increasing in the knowledge of God; being strengthened with all power, according to his glorious might, for all endurance and patience with joy...

Every Christian has a calling. We did not receive the free gift of salvation to hide it or focus on personal blessing. We are blessed to be a blessing.

God has uniquely created every person that walks on Earth with individual personalities, thinking capacities, aptitudes, and abilities. It is the believer's responsibility to steward the gift of salvation, their unique talents, and the call of God to be used for His Kingdom's purposes.

Bearing spiritual fruit requires intentional equipping, growth in wisdom, godly living, and a servant's heart to do the will of God. How are you intentionally equipping yourself to bear maximum fruit for God's Kingdom? In what ways are you bearing spiritual fruit, being used of God for His purposes? How can you move forward to increase your knowledge and service to the King?

_____
_____
_____
_____
_____
_____

My thoughts…

I know that God did not bring me back to life just to enjoy the next few decades. I know Jesus sent me back because I had not finished the tasks He has ordained me to do.

Bearing eternal fruit is my mission. Eternal fruit includes God using me to share the Good News about WHO Jesus is and WHAT He has done for all mankind. It also means encouraging my brothers and sisters about what I have personally witnessed - the absolute reality of Jesus and Heaven! I believe it is why God allowed my body to be dead for so long - twenty-seven minutes! And why it was all medically documented - to strengthen my witness to a skeptical world of the existence of God and Heaven.

I want to be faithful. I want to hear Jesus say, "Well done, good and faithful servant!". To be fruitful, I know I have to stay planted in good soil, put down deep roots, and be fed in order to grow. I remain committed to a local church, devoted to being a student of God's Word, and faithful in prayer. I have a group of wise, mature Christian mentors that I have invited to speak into my life.

I believe that this great blessing of dying, going to Heaven, seeing Jesus, and being restored to life comes with great responsibility. I want to steward this gift faithfully so that I can be fully pleasing to Him, bearing fruit in every good work!

Proverbs 3:5-6 ESV
Trust in the Lord with all your heart, and do not lean on your own understanding. In all your ways acknowledge him, and he will make straight your paths.

King Solomon wrote this Proverb. Solomon asked God for wisdom to distinguish between right and wrong, and God gave him a "wise and discerning heart" (1 Kings 3:12). Notice that Solomon uses the word "all" twice in this passage. Fully trust in the Lord and fully acknowledge (recognize and obey) Him.

The passage comes with a promise for those who embrace fully trusting and fully obeying God. The promise is that God will make straight paths for the faithful follower. A straight path refers to a path that He makes a way for us - guiding and directing us so that we do not get lost on paths He never intended us to follow.

Are you fully trusting and acknowledging God in your life? If so, you can be confident that He is going before you, at times making a way where there seems to be no way. Rest and trust in His direction. Identify areas that you need to fully trust God and acknowledge Him, then surrender them to Him in prayer.

_____
_____
_____
_____
_____
_____
_____

My thoughts…

From the world's perspective, no one would ever, AND could NEVER imagine, that twenty-seven minutes without a breath and without a heartbeat would allow the outcome of MY LIFE….to be saved and healed….. To survive sudden cardiac arrest…

The incredible sovereignty of who YOU are, and the magnificent way You showed Yourself on February 12, 2018, is still astounding, hard to comprehend, and impossible for human hearts to understand and believe…

BUT IN YOU ALONE, IT IS REAL!!!!

Thank you for the years, months, weeks, days, hours, minutes, and seconds You continue to show Yourself. I am in AWE of You, as I spend time with You in the mornings and through my days and see Your face right before me!

As I spend time with You in prayer and in Your Word, I know that You strengthen me. I am renewed to delight in Your will and walk in Your ways for Your glorious purposes. May Your will be done in and through me today.

Isaiah 40:31 ESV
...But they who wait for the Lord shall renew their strength; they shall mount up with wings like eagles; they shall run and not be weary; they shall walk and not faint.

We live in a fallen world in vessels made of clay. Our hearts and minds grow weary. To have the strength and wisdom needed to interact in a godly manner, we must move into God's Presence daily.

Without God renewing our strength, we simply rely on our own finite abilities and energy. The end results of what we do will be human. If we want God's best, what we think, say, and do must be infused with His direction, wisdom, and anointing. This only comes from time spent in His Presence.

Mounting up with wings like eagles symbolizes strength and perspective gained through time in the Word and prayer. Identify times you are prone to move in your own strength and wisdom. Describe an action plan to intentionally wait on the Lord for direction, understanding, and anointing.

_____
_____
_____
_____
_____
_____
_____
_____
_____
_____
_____

My thoughts…

Lord,

Thank you for relentlessly pursuing me….FOR TEACHING ME TO TRUST IN YOUR STRENGTH ALONE!!! Not mine…but Yours, oh Lord! My heart's desire is to trust You in ALL things. Still, sometimes I get weary with day-to-day life challenges, work, kids, schedules, physical demands, and emotional roller coasters.

As You have given me LIFE on this earth once again after 2/12/18, I pray that my (at times) weary and tired heart continues to run to the depth, the strength, the wisdom, and the accuracy of Your Word!

Somehow, You've given me an ability in my body to have ALOT of energy…. even without drinking coffee every day 😂 (as my Brian and family would say!) I still crave 5 AM gym workouts and early morning hikes to see the sunrise!!

BUT sometimes I'm just simply weary in my heart and mind….. BUT….. I find incredible strength in You…. YOUR GOSPEL IS MY HOPE, YOUR GOSPEL IS MY GUIDE, YOUR GOSPEL IS MY TRUTH!

Your words continue to lead me to the cross and train me to run without growing weary… Thank you that in my time with You, I am strengthened and EQUIPPED for anything You walk me through today!!!

Galatians 6:8b-9 ESV

...The one who sows to the Spirit will from the Spirit reap eternal life. And let us not grow weary of doing good, for in due season we will reap, if we do not give up.

The Apostle Paul wrote with a firm tone to the Church in Galatia. Many were deserting the truths of the Gospel, accepting the teaching that living according to their lusts was permissible. He was calling for commitment in clinging to the Truth and perseverance to living it out.

Paul admonished the believers, reminding them that we will all stand before God to account for our service to Him, reaping the reward for being faithful and obedient.

There is no time or room for the follower of Christ to be distracted by things of the world, no matter how difficult. Sickness, wars, and rumors of wars, conflict between family members - all of this and more was predicted as we draw closer to the return of Jesus. In what ways are you exercising endurance - faithfully serving despite difficulties? In what ways have you held back? Articulate ways to move forward, serving in faith despite emotion and circumstance.

_____
_____
_____
_____
_____
_____
_____
_____
_____

Jesus speaking to me...

"If you COMPLETELY trust me, you can ENDURE, TINA.... Continue deeply trusting Me and walking closely with Me amid uncertainties."

Keep on seeing the good in all I am doing in your life and with those around you..... Even in pain, hurt, fear, sadness, loss, uncertainty, and the oppression of today's world, because I GIVE YOU HOPE AND LIFE!

Endure through the challenges of each day and the joys that come in the mornings. As you know, I provide all you need.

FOCUS AND SETTLE IN YOUR MIND AND HEART ON THE HOPE OF ME..... Not what is going on in this world. ENDURE the difficulties because you are chosen, and remember My faithfulness, kindness, and goodness to you always!"

My thoughts...

I need to practice ENDURANCE during the pandemic. I need to battle through emotions to the truth that God is ALWAYS AND FOREVER on the throne, and I am called to serve Him faithfully regardless of circumstance!!!!

1 Peter 2:9 ESV

But you are a chosen race, a royal priesthood, a holy nation, a people for his own possession, that you may proclaim the excellencies of him who called you out of darkness into his marvelous light.

The Apostle Peter wrote to the early Church scattered through Asia Minor. They were suffering persecution under Nero's reign of terror. He reminded them of the miraculous gift and honor of being called and chosen to bear witness of Jesus, the Light of the World.

Identity in Christ means being a son or daughter of the King. It is a position of royalty that brings both great honor and great responsibility. As a result of being bestowed the status of royalty - sons and daughters - God expects us to live as His children. We are called to courageous obedience to our Heavenly Father - to represent Him well with our lives and with our life witness to Who He is. Do you fully grasp the incredible gift of your identity in Christ? Have you embraced the calling that accompanies the gift? Describe your identity and calling in light of who God says you are.

_____
_____
_____
_____
_____
_____
_____
_____
_____

My thoughts...

Our identity is in CHRIST ALONE.... not our marriages, family status, careers, material status, or accomplishments.

Who am I? A wife, a mother, a sister, a daughter, an employee... Yet if I described myself by these relationships, the most IMPORTANT relationship that determines how I interact in every other relationship would be missing.

I am a daughter of the King of Kings, a servant of the most high God, a follower of Jesus, forgiven, called, and purposed for the works He determined for me before I was born. I have a destiny, a mission, and a responsibility. I am gifted by God to fulfill His purposes for me.

My relationship with Jesus equips me to be a loving wife and mother, a good sister and daughter, and a diligent employee. It also empowers me to proclaim the truth of WHO Jesus is and WHAT He has done for me - and this is my purpose. He chose me to faithfully proclaim His marvelous light, which I have seen with my own eyes as an act of His great grace.

In Christ alone, through His strength and power, I am equipped to do and be all He calls me to. And, I will never stop sharing about the reality of Jesus and the truth of Heaven so that others might be called out of darkness to His marvelous light!

John 15:12-13 ESV
"This is my commandment, that you love one another as I have loved you. Greater love has no one than this, that someone lay down his life for his friends.

In John chapter 15, Jesus is having an intimate conversation with His disciples, preparing them for the time when He would no longer be with them. After the crucifixion and resurrection of Jesus, tremendous persecution broke out in Jerusalem against followers of "The Way". Betrayal, desertion, martyrdom - the disciples would face all of this, and Jesus already knew it.

He reminded them of the strength and encouragement that comes from deeply loving each other. Today, God gives us a spouse, brother or sister in Christ. We need one another and are called to deeply love those we walk with.

Marriage, friendships, family - sowing sacrificial love into these relationships, loving as Christ loves us, takes intentionality. Sowing brings blessed reaping. You will reap the benefits of strong relationships that bring comfort and strength in times of challenge. In what ways are you intentionally nurturing your marriage, family, and friendships to walk together in faith?

_____
_____
_____
_____
_____
_____
_____
_____

My thoughts...

Every day I PRAISE YOU AND THANK YOU so sincerely and deeply for the marriage and life with Brian that You've given to us!! I cry out in tears, as I am journaling with You right now, with an unbelievable, overwhelming sense of gratefulness for my marriage to Brian for over thirty-four years!

Thank you, Heavenly Father... You orchestrated and designed it to be an amazing, life giving gift... How could we have even known that on February 12, 2018, in Your sovereignty and kindness, You planned for Brian to help save my life? My husband performed CPR on me... it was the most traumatic and life-altering day of his life. He saw me turn blue, eyes rolled back, not breathing...

Marriage is not for the faint hearted. We do harder things than we ever imagined through Your Strength! Richer or poorer, in sickness and in health, has been a full reality for Brian. He watched me die before his eyes..... battled through mountains of hospital bills... We have been through triumphs and tragedies. And you GOD, have continued to honor, bless and strengthen our marriage, to move through the hard things.

Thank you God, for allowing Brian to see how this MIRACLE story has been used to encourage others to love and know Jesus and love each other well, every day, as if it's our last!! Talk about "love in action" from the incredible, amazing husband You have blessed me with, for the past thirty-four years!!

Matthew 6:9-13 ESV

"Pray then like this: Our Father in heaven, hallowed be your name. Your kingdom come, your will be done, on earth as it is in heaven. Give us this day our daily bread, and forgive us our debts, as we also have forgiven our debtors. And lead us not into temptation, but deliver us from evil."

Matthew chapter 6 is part of the Sermon on the Mount. Jesus sat down on a hillside to teach His disciples. Crowds gathered, astonished as His wisdom to speak into their anxious minds and hearts, showing them a better way.

Today, His Words still resonate with compassionate understanding of our human frailties. The Lord's Prayer, as the above passage is referred to, is Jesus' instruction on how to pray - recognizing God as sovereign, surrendering our will to His, trusting Him for daily provision, walking in forgiveness, and resisting temptation. Simple, powerful, and profound. This prayer is immensely helpful in one day at a time living - getting up, surrendering the day, trusting God, and going forward in faith that His grace is enough. What part of this prayer is most difficult for you to practice on a day to day basis? Describe practical ways to apply the day to day principles in this prayer: (ex: viewing financial provision as daily instead of worrying about the future).

_____
_____
_____
_____
_____
_____
_____

My thoughts...

After I returned from Heaven, the phrase "Your Kingdom" meant something different to me than it did before. I guess I had never thought about God being the King that ruled an actual Kingdom from His throne and that He would speak and His will would be fulfilled perfectly there. I think in pictures, so after seeing the Gates of Heaven, I could imagine what was beyond. The throne, the altar, angels, and saints worship Him - a picture of perfect harmony and right order.

We don't have perfect harmony or biblical order in this fallen world. But, we can order OUR OWN LIVES according to God's Kingdom values. When we prioritize our lives according to His Kingdom, His harmony reigns in our hearts and home.

Brian and I don't see day-to-day life the same anymore. Financial stressors don't cause us fear. We know Who meets our needs. And, we loved our family deeply before I died, but now how we prioritize our family has changed. We don't wait to have family time until "everything is done" - we schedule it as a most important priority.

We also don't hold grudges - daily forgiveness happens in our household because you never know when, well... someone could die, and we could regret our last words. Time is too short - literally - and living intentionally one day at a time with Kingdom priorities reaps more benefits than I could ever have imagined.

Matthew 6:19-21 ESV

"Do not lay up for yourselves treasures on earth, where moth and rust destroy and where thieves break in and steal, but lay up for yourselves treasures in heaven, where neither moth nor rust destroys and where thieves do not break in and steal. For where your treasure is, there your heart will be also."

Living in a material world, seeing images of luxurious lifestyles, fabulous vacations, perfect families…. We are bombarded constantly with messaging designed to stir up a desire for more. Like Eve in the Garden, it's easy to believe the lie that we need what we don't have.

Being wealthy is not a sin - God blessed Job with wealth because He knew Job would wisely steward what he was given. The rich young ruler who came to Jesus was a different story. Although sad, he refused Jesus' invitation to follow Him, choosing his great wealth instead. Jesus said it was easier for a camel to go through the eye of a needle than a rich man to get into Heaven. Why? Possessions are not inherently evil, but placing wealth above the pursuit of God is. Does what you own hinder God's call on your life? Do you demonstrate faithful stewardship by tithing to your local church? Describe biblical priorities for the material possessions God has given you.

_____
_____
_____
_____
_____
_____
_____

My thoughts…

After I died and the Lord graciously brought me back to life, the medical bills piled up rapidly. The ambulance, the emergency room, the intensive care unit… All of the procedures and specialists, and then all of the outpatient treatment once I was discharged…

Brian and I have never been people that sought wealth. We have always worked hard and lived within our means. We just absolutely were not prepared for the onslaught of bills! Knowing God absolutely orchestrated this entire situation, we prayed and asked for direction.

Because we knew that Jesus sent me back to testify to the truth of who He is and the reality of Heaven, the calling had to become the first priority. We decided to sell our home to pay the bills, knowing that when we put Him first, He is always faithful to provide.

Downsizing to a smaller home and simpler lifestyle was hard - I loved the beauty of our home and raising our children there! But, as difficult as it was, there was a peace about priorities.

Having seen the beauty of Heaven helped me focus on eternal priorities. It enables us to put people and ministry above things and places. And now, the day-to-day joy I experience from being used for His service is worth any sacrifice, big or small! The shift to heavenly priorities is so very worth it!!

Matthew 22:37-40 ESV

"Teacher, which is the great commandment in the Law?" And he said to him, "You shall love the Lord your God with all your heart and with all your soul and with all your mind. This is the great and first commandment. And a second is like it: You shall love your neighbor as yourself. On these two commandments depend all the Law and the Prophets."

When we comprehend what God's immeasurable love towards us really means, how He sees us, and all He has done for us, we acknowledge a debt we owe that can never be repaid. The Good News is that He doesn't ask us to! God loves us so much that He sacrificed His only Son to save us from ourselves. Jesus the Son graciously shared the immense love of the Father towards us - His mercy, goodness, and grace - a gift we could never deserve or earn.

As we get to know God better through His Word and time in prayer, our love for Him grows. We gain the understanding that He is Truth, Love, All-Powerful, Everywhere! He knows everything and loves us still! How could we not love Him with all of our being? When we are in love with God, it fills us to overflowing, equipping us to love others as we are commanded. Does passion for God fill your heart, mind, and soul? Does it overflow in loving others? How can you deepen your love for God and love for others?

_____
_____
_____
_____
_____

My thoughts…

I have been a woman of faith for many years, and have loved God for as long as I can remember. He wired me to love people - I am really a people person! I love being around all kinds of people, hearing their stories, and helping where I can.

However, loving God with my heart, soul, and mind feels different now. It is all-encompassing! It's hard to describe because I believe I fully loved God before I died. It's just that my mind was not filled with thoughts of Jesus and Heaven like it is now!

Perhaps Jesus is more tangible to me now - I can see Jesus' face in my mind when I tell Him I love Him! Someone showed me a painting Akiane Kramarik created at age eight. She painted it after Jesus spoke to her when she was four, encouraging her to draw and paint her visions, one of which was Him. When I saw the picture, it took my breath away! Jesus looks like her portrait!! The dark hair, intense eyes, compassion in His glance. I saw the painting and began weeping tears of joy. I said, 'It's Him!!".

All I can say is that knowing how real, beautiful, compassionate, and merciful He is, I love Him with every fiber of my heart, soul, and mind! I will serve Him with all of my strength. And, My love for Him is spilling over, flooding out of me to love and serve others. I am absolutely compelled to love because I am loved by Him!

John 20:27-29 ESV
Then he said to Thomas, "Put your finger here, and see my hands; and put out your hand, and place it in my side. Do not disbelieve, but believe." Thomas answered him, "My Lord and my God!" Jesus said to him, "Have you believed because you have seen me? Blessed are those who have not seen and yet have believed."

The disciples Jesus called were all martyred, except for the Apostle John (and Judas). They spent three years with Jesus, witnessing miracle after miracle, listening to His teaching, being discipled by Him. On the other hand, Paul did not know Jesus and persecuted Christians. He met Jesus a different way - in a blinding vision! Jesus was so tangible to Paul that he gave up everything to serve and obey Him, eventually becoming a martyr for his faith.

One does not have to see Jesus in person to know Him personally. When Jesus ascended to Heaven, He promised that His Father would send the Helper, the Holy Spirit, to reveal Truth (John 14:28). The Holy Spirit brings Scripture to life, enabling us to comprehend God's Truth (Hebrews 4:12). God also speaks in visions (Paul's conversion), miracles (Paul raised Eutychus from the dead - Acts 20:10), and through His faithful witnesses who proclaim His reality! How do YOU know that God, Jesus, Heaven, the Holy Spirit, and Scripture are real? Describe your witness below.

_____
_____
_____
_____
_____
_____

My thoughts…

How blessed I am to have died! I know that sounds weird. But I wouldn't trade dying for anything! How many of us would give up our own lives if it would ensure our children's salvation? And while that method doesn't work with God… the idea of dying so that I can testify to the reality of Heaven and Jesus so that others can find faith and be strengthened in faith is totally worth it!

Of course, the experience in Heaven was so indescribably joyous I wouldn't trade it for anything this world has to offer! But, I know that Jesus did not give me this blessing just so I could hoard the joy. This incredible blessing is so that I can be a blessing.

Most people don't die and come back to life. Most people don't go to Heaven, see Jesus, and then have their bodies start functioning again. I mean, my ER nurse was ready to sign the paperwork so my organs could be donated!

Jesus said blessed are you who haven't seen and yet believe! God is real, Heaven is real, eternity is real, the Bible is real… Miracles are real, and God is with us! It's all real, and while you might not see it for yourself until He takes you into eternity, I can assure you with absolute certainty how real it all is!

I know some cynics don't believe me. It's why I think God allowed every moment of the twenty-seven minutes my body was dead to be medically documented and have medical professionals witness to the fact that I died and came back to life. Be encouraged! It's ALL REAL! I'm living, breathing proof.

Revelation 21: 3-4 ESV

And I heard a loud voice from the throne saying, "Behold, the dwelling place of God is with man. He will dwell with them, and they will be his people, and God himself will be with them as their God. 4 He will wipe away every tear from their eyes, and death shall be no more, neither shall there be mourning, nor crying, nor pain anymore, for the former things have passed away."

The above passage is a beautiful reminder of what it will be like to be with our Heavenly Father for eternity! Those that pass from this life to the next are experiencing His complete peace and rest right now!.

We embrace the reality of Heaven and that one day, Jesus will return again for those that remain. He will create a new Heaven and new earth. Those who love Him will dwell in its' splendor, marvelling at its' wonders and rejoicing that there is no more sickness, death, sin… living in pure joy without a trace of the old, fallen world!

Study Scripture to understand what Heaven looks like and the new Heaven and Earth that are coming. God gives us a sneak peek into the wonders that await us through His Word. Write down specific Scriptures that describe Heaven now and the new Heaven and Earth that God will create. Remind yourself of the wonders that await when He calls you to Himself so that you don't walk in fear or grief!

_____

_____

_____

_____

_____

_____

_____

My thoughts…

These past two years have been difficult for so many people. I have lost loved ones and seen the emotional impact of COVID - grief, fear, depression…

I genuinely believe that the message God has given me to share after meeting Jesus in Heaven can help so many who have struggled so much. Because I know what it feels like to die and the incredible experience of being with Jesus in Heaven, I am really not afraid of death anymore. And the truth is, I am SO VERY EXCITED to spend eternity in Heaven with Jesus!

Losing people we love is always heartbreaking. Missing them here on earth is part of being human. But those who have gone to be with Jesus are not struggling like we struggle. They are experiencing the absolute JOY of Heaven, overwhelmed by its' beauty, filled with its' peace, and singing at the top of their lungs, worshipping the God of the Universe! No more sickness, pain, heartache - just pure joy! I have a very clear picture of this in my mind now, and while my heart still misses loved ones, I am so very blessed because I know what they get to see and experience, and it is AMAZING!!

Staying focused on the reality of Heaven, Jesus, and the wonders that await us all steadies me, fills me with strength when I am weary, and peace when I am troubled. I know beyond a shadow of a doubt that pressing on towards our eternal destiny is worth everything!

Revelation 3:20-22 ESV
"Behold, I stand at the door and knock. If anyone hears My voice and opens the door, I will come in to him and eat with him, and he with Me. The one who conquers, I will grant him to sit with Me on my throne, as I also conquered and sat down with my Father on His throne. He who has an ear, let him hear what the Spirit says to the churches.'"

Fellowship with Jesus and victory through Him! It is the offer Jesus made to the seven churches in the book of Revelation experiencing persecution. By this time, the Apostle John was an old man exiled to the island of Patmos as a prisoner of the Roman Empire. Jesus appeared to John in a marvelous vision that became the Book of Revelation. It was written to remind believers that Jesus was present to strengthen them to stand firm in faith, overcome the world, and enter eternity to rule and reign with Him.

The offer of a personal relationship with Jesus was not just for the persecuted churches of Asia. It is the offer He extends to all mankind. Are you actively sharing His incredible offer? How can you be bolder in sharing this amazing truth that Jesus is waiting with open arms?

_____

_____

_____

_____

_____

_____

_____

_____

My thoughts…

I know how loving our Heavenly Father is. He loves us more than we can comprehend. I can't imagine His grief and pain as He watched His Son suffer - beaten, spit on, nailed to a cross to suffocate to death when He had done nothing wrong! And Jesus! When I kneel in my mind at the foot of the cross, holding His feet with the nail holes, I am overwhelmed by His love - that He was willing to suffer and die such a horrible death to save me!

I know that I am a sinner only saved by God's amazing love and mercy. What is even more overwhelming to me is that not only was His incredible sacrifice made on my behalf, but now He calls me His friend. He desires an active, authentic relationship with Him. Me! He wants to be with me! How could I ever deny that kind of love? Or the incredible offer of being in a loving relationship that gives me strength, peace, joy, wisdom, and direction while I'm in this fallen world?

I know with certainty that if people seek Jesus, they will find Him. He is always waiting with open arms, just like He did with me in Heaven! He held out His arms to me when I saw Him! He wants to embrace all that will come to Him and give them the same gifts He has given me!

I pray for God to give me His Words when I share with others. I want to vividly express just how VERY REAL this all is and that it is worth everything to be in a living, loving relationship with Jesus for eternity!

Revelation 22:1-5 ESV

Then the angel showed me the river of the water of life, as clear as crystal, flowing from the throne of God and of the Lamb down the middle of the great street of the city. On each side of the river stood the tree of life, bearing twelve crops of fruit, yielding its fruit every month. And the leaves of the tree are for the healing of the nations. No longer will there be any curse. The throne of God and of the Lamb will be in the city, and his servants will serve him. They will see his face, and his name will be on their foreheads. There will be no more night. They will not need the light of a lamp or the light of the sun, for the Lord God will give them light. And they will reign for ever and ever.

The verses above describe the Holy City, the New Jerusalem, which God prepares for His bride - followers of Jesus the Messiah. No more death, grief, sin, or separation from God. His Kingdom will have come - God will dwell among His people. Nothing impure can enter this city - it will remain holy, filled with the glory of God that illuminates it! The city is described with dazzling splendor in Revelation chapters 21 and 22. God, in His mercy, gave us revelation of the future to strengthen us in the here and now. In what ways are you strengthened by the description of the New Jerusalem where believers will dwell for eternity?

_____
_____
_____
_____
_____
_____
_____

My thoughts…

WOW!! Just WOW! Jesus, in His incredible love, meeting me in Heaven! I didn't actually enter but stood outside of the gates of Heaven. The little bit I saw was overwhelmingly beautiful - so much so that my heart longs for Heaven and to be in the Presence of Jesus!

What amazes me is that it is going to get BETTER! I was so filled with wonder, joy, peace, and love that it seems impossible to me that eternity will be better than what I experienced, but God's Word says it does!

I am now such a student of God's Word! Before I died, I studied my Bible, but now it feels like I drink in every Word - it is indeed living water that quenches my thirsty soul.

Scripture has so much to say about what Heaven is like. And there are many specifics in the Book of Revelation about what it will be like when Jesus returns and the new Heaven and new earth come down. It really is like the Garden of Eden restored - everything perfect, with God Himself as the Light and darkness wholly dispelled.

This is where we will live for all of eternity. It's almost too good to believe. But… guess what?? It's real, it's true, and it is going to be INCREDIBLE! I pray your heart is filled with joyful hope at what awaits us. Let the weariness fade away, and rest in His promises of making everything new.

John 14:1-4 ESV

"Let not your hearts be troubled. Believe in God; believe also in Me. In my Father's house are many rooms. If it were not so, would I have told you that I go to prepare a place for you? And if I go and prepare a place for you, I will come again and will take you to Myself, that where I am you may be also. And you know the way to where I am going."

In the above passage, Jesus was comforting His disciples as His earthly ministry was coming to a close, preparing them for His return to His Father in Heaven.

Jesus gives the disciples specifics about preparing a dwelling place for them in Heaven. The Greek word is "*mone*" and literally translated means abode. The focus was not on giant mansions in the sky but rather the disciples dwelling with Jesus in Heaven. This is the point believers can take the most comfort from. Jesus has prepared a place for His followers, will return for each one, and take us there Himself when it is time.

Death is a transition from living in a fallen world with a decaying earthly body to living for eternity in the Presence of Almighty God. We will not make the transition from this life to the next alone - our Savior will come and get us! How does this biblical truth impact your understanding of the death experience? In what ways do you need to change your thinking to match the biblical reality of death?

_____

_____

_____

_____

_____

_____

My thoughts…

I have been given another chance at life. Not many people are given the gift of dying and then living again. It was not dying that changed me. Everybody will die. Not everybody will go to Heaven and be with Jesus.

So few have died and now have the opportunity to share about the experience of death. I can tell you that my body was dead, but my spirit was truly alive in Christ!

I think Christians who fear death are not aware of how much Jesus prepares us! So much encouragement to not be afraid, so many beautiful descriptions of the glorious eternal life that awaits us! And yet, so many remain fearful.

Maybe it is not death that Christians are afraid of. Perhaps it is the suffering that precedes death that scares us. All I know is the truth that no matter WHAT we experience, Jesus promises to never leave or forsake us! He even promised we would not die alone. I also know how loving, kind, and full of mercy our Heavenly Father is. How He carries us when we are weak, comforts us when we are hurting, and cherishes us when we feel alone. How could the journey into His Presence be any different?

Don't let your heart be troubled. He is Emmanuel - God With Us! He will not leave or forsake us. He loves us. We are precious in His sight. Rest in His provision and Presence. Take courage! Heaven… it's REAL, and the arms of Jesus are stretched out to draw you in close - now and for eternity.

Made in the USA
Las Vegas, NV
20 January 2024

84660722R00037